I Forgive You

Also by Robert Chafe

Robert Chafe: Two Plays
Afterimage
Under Wraps
Oil and Water
The Colony of Unrequited Dreams
Between Breaths
Everybody Just C@lm the F#ck Down

I Forgive You

Scott Jones &
Robert Chafe

Playwrights Canada Press
Toronto

First edition: June 2024
Printed and bound in Canada by Rapido Books, Montreal

Jacket art and design by Tobias Diuk
Photo of Scott Jones by Tora Chirilă
Photo of Robert Chafe by Ritche Perez

Playwrights Canada Press
202-269 Richmond St. W., Toronto, ON M5V 1X1
416.703.0013 | info@playwrightscanada.com | www.playwrightscanada.com

For professional or amateur production rights, please contact:
Meaghan Denomme, GGA
250 The Esplanade, Suite 304, Toronto, ON M5A 1J2
416-928-0299 x5 | meaghan@ggagency.ca | www.ggagency.ca

LIBRARY AND ARCHIVES CANADA CATALOGUING IN PUBLICATION
Title: I forgive you / Scott Jones & Robert Chafe.
Names: Jones, Scott (Filmmaker), author. | Chafe, Robert, author.
Identifiers: Canadiana (print) 20240321049 | Canadiana (ebook) 20240321103 | ISBN 9780369104984 (softcover) | ISBN 9780369104991 (PDF) | ISBN 9780369105004 (EPUB)
Subjects: LCGFT: Drama.
Classification: LCC PS8619.O53385 I2 2024 | DDC C812/.6—dc23

Playwrights Canada Press staff work across Turtle Island, on Treaty 7, Treaty 13, and Treaty 20 territories, which are the current and ancestral homes of the Anishinaabe Nations (Ojibwe / Chippewa, Odawa, Potawatomi, Algonquin, Saulteaux, Nipissing, and Mississauga / Michi Saagiig), the Blackfoot Confederacy (Kainai, Piikani, and Siksika), nêhiyaw, Sioux, Stoney Nakoda, Tsuut'ina, Wendat, and members of the Haudenosaunee Confederacy (Mohawk, Oneida, Onondaga, Cayuga, Seneca, and Tuscarora), as well as Metis and Inuit peoples. It always was and always will be Indigenous land.

We acknowledge the financial support of the Canada Council for the Arts, the Ontario Arts Council (OAC), Ontario Creates, the Government of Ontario, and the Government of Canada for our publishing activities.

Canada Council for the Arts | Conseil des arts du Canada
ONTARIO ARTS COUNCIL
CONSEIL DES ARTS DE L'ONTARIO
an Ontario government agency
un organisme du gouvernement de l'Ontario
ONTARIO CREATES | ONTARIO CRÉATIF
Canada
Ontario

I would like to dedicate this work to my mother, Lois, to my grandmother, Stella, and to my sisters, Cara, Sherise, and Gabrielle.

Mom, thank you for always allowing me to be me. Your love continues to help me grow as a person and recover from the unthinkable. Gramma, thank you for staying so close and watching over me that night.

I carry each of you in my heart and soul forever. For you are a part of my very existence on Earth and in the next life as well.

—Scott

Foreword

By Sarah Garton Stanley (SGS)

Things sometimes begin this way, with a question or a quest. This one was both. "There is this guy. His name is Scott Jones. Have you heard of him?" This was from director Jillian Keiley. I had. "I am hoping to meet with him and see if he would be open to Artistic Fraud creating a new show about his extraordinary story." The "story" had gone viral. As a young man, Scott was the victim of a horrendous hate crime, and at the trial instead of reading the expected victim impact statement, he forgave the man who had assaulted him. Who does that? This question became the root from which everything blossomed in this work co-written by Scott and Robert Chafe. But "that story" quickly became suspect as the basis for a play. After all, it wasn't a story. It was a moment in time that arose from actions enacted on a person without cause or warning. A moment that stands between Scott's actions in a courtroom and my writing this foreword now.

There are too many unique aspects to this extraordinary piece of live theatre to examine them all. Yet what stands above the crowd of wonders is how every word belongs to Scott. Through years made even more lengthy by a pandemic, Scott and Robert would meet and talk. They met in person, sometimes with Jill Keiley and me present; they met on Zoom; they met over the phone. The text from those discussions was transcribed and, with other writings of Scott's, formed the material from which this two-act play emerged. The music that Scott heard while spending unthinkable amounts of time in the hospital became the material that the choir of young people sing. And the chronology of Scott's life events formed the backbone of the play's trajectory. Every word belongs to Scott.

I Forgive You is an incomplete testimony of what happened and a testament to the power of creativity and collaboration to loosen the calcification of pain that hardens around events. Scott has always been an extraordinary artist. The making of this work brought together a level of artistry that is rare. A meeting place between Scott, the events of Scott's life, Robert, and a relationship forged between these two artistic forces, and the rest of us, all offering what we could to the root question: Who does that? And why?

Because of Scott we are all on this quest to contemplate the potential for forgiveness and the attendant impossibility of it. The tension in this play lives between these two points. And so too does the hope. And that, the quest for, the possibility of (and the impossibility always) is the quest.

Director, dramaturg, and creator Sarah Garton Stanley (SGS) is Vice President of Programming at Arts Commons in Calgary. She is originally from Montreal, and was previously Artistic Producer of the National Creation Fund at Canada's National Arts Centre, founding Artistic Director of SpiderWebShow, co-founder of FOLDA, Associate Artistic Director for English Theatre (NAC), and Artistic Director of Buddies in Bad Times Theatre. She has been the recipient of the Literary Managers and Dramaturgs of the Americas's Elliott Hayes Award, a Manitoba Theatre Award for best direction, and an Honorary Member Award from the Canadian Association for Theatre Research. SGS holds a Ph.D. in Cultural Studies from Queen's University and in 2020 she and her partner became co-stewards of the legendary Birchdale in Nova Scotia. SGS is co-author of Manifesto for Now *with Owais Lightwalla.*

I Forgive You was first produced by Artistic Fraud at the Arts & Culture Centre in St. John's, Newfoundland, on August 25, 2022, with the following cast and creative team:

Character One: Jeff Ho
Character Two: Nathan Carroll
Scott: Scott Jones
The Child: Lennox Blue Powell
Children's Choir: Ella Ball, Anthony Donnan, Emmajane Donnan, Annabelle Edmunds-Ramsay, Josie Ellis, Liam Fowler, Cohen Gardner-Hedges, Isabella Hallett, Lily Hallett, Madeline Lomholt-Mortensen, Ayeesha Mekawy, Jane Osmond, Lauren Patten, Mya Rogers, Eliza Somers, Aoife Strand, and Allison Walsh
Understudy: Santiago Guzmán

Director: Jillian Keiley
Assistant Director: Sharon King-Campbell
Musical Director: Kellie Walsh
Associate Musical Director: Jennifer Hart
Performance Conductor: Scott Jones
Composer: Sigur Rós
Music Arrangement: Ingi Garðar Erlendsson
Movement Director: Christopher House
Associate Movement Director: Josh Murphy
Production Dramaturge: Sarah Garton Stanley
Additional Dramaturgy: Jeff Ho and Nathan Carroll
Set & Costume Designer: Alison Helmer
Sound Designer: Don Ellis
Lighting Designer: Bonnie Beecher
Stage Manager: Kai-Yueh Chen
Assistant Stage Manager: Tiff Roberts

Scenic Painter: Sara Dorey
Technical Director: Brian Kenny
Producer: Patrick Foran
Associate Producer: Crystal Laffoley
Interlocutor: April Hubbard
Directing Shadow: Azal Dosanjh
Directing Protegé: Paul David Power
Marketing & Communications: Robyn Vivian
Child Minder: Veronica Quinn

In March 2023, Artistic Fraud's production was remounted and presented by the National Arts Centre's English Theatre in the Azrieli Studio, Ottawa, with the following artists joining the production:

Children's Choir: Michèle Barker, Emma Barrette, Leah Christie, Elliott Doulet, Tamara Emond, Alexia Ferrand, César Gauthier, Adrian Grinberg-Chambers, Maeve Hickey, Annie Hume, Sarah Hume, Hanan Kaekiza, Clémence Kanyoka, Melina Kovacheff, Eponine Lee, Sophie Letcher, Carmen Rose Nicholson, Bethany Olszewski, Maya Peters, Lennox Blue Powell, Noah Scharr, and Henri Trépanier

Ottawa Musical Director: Robert Filion
Ottawa Associate Musical Director: Theresa Clarke
Technical Director: Reg Hoskins
Associate Lighting Designer: Jeff Pybus
Interlocutor: Graham Scott
Assistant Stage Manager: Arielle Voght
Child Minders: Nathan McConnell, Krista Fowler, and Jessica Murphy
Disability Advocates: Harry Brown and Kristen Williams
Marketing & Communications: Emma Cole

Music

Below are the musical selections (by Sigur Rós, arranged by Ingi Garðar Erlendsson) and corresponding scenes as performed during Artistic Fraud's production of *I Forgive You* at the Arts and Culture Centre, St. John's, Newfoundland, and the National Arts Centre, Ottawa, Ontario.

Act One

Victim Impact Statement
"Fljótavík"

Verbatim
"Með Blóðnasir"

I'm Trying to Tell You Something
"Inní mér syngur vitleysingur" (excerpt)

I Want to Do This
"Viðrar vel til loftárása"

Summer of Scott
"Inní mér syngur vitleysingur"

We Both Had Just Moved Back
"Fjögur píanó"

What's So Gay
"Dauðalogn"

Five Months
"Straumnes" and "Fljótavík"

Don't Be Afraid
"Ára bátur"

Dear Scott
"Fjögur pianó"

This Story
"Choral Drone/Cluster" based on "Varúð"
(**unison drone:** B-flat 4; **two-note cluster:** B-flat 4 + C 5; **three-note cluster:** B-flat 4 + C 5 + D-flat 5)

Act Two

Before and After
"Aria" (featuring *Goldberg Variations BWV988* by J. S. Bach)

Forgiveness
"Debata mandire"

Hi Shane
"Varúð"

Flamboyant
"Ára bátur" (excerpt, B section)

He's Up For It
"Varðeldur" and "Untitled #1—Vaka"

Mersey River
"Andvari"

Do You Forgive Him?
"Straumnes II"

The Same Person
"Untitled #3—Samskeyti"

Notes On Production

I Forgive You was conceived as a verbatim piece backed by the presence and music of a live youth choir. All of the text in the piece was collected, edited, and assembled by Scott and Robert. The first-person text was then split between two actors who relay the story in the presence of Scott himself. Scott conducted the choir on stage during every performance as they performed selections by Sigur Rós, adapted for piano and choir by Ingi Garðar Erlendsson. The choir sang mostly in a semicircle formation centre stage, either seated or standing, with choreographed scenes as an exception. Two keyboards were positioned at each end of the ensemble's semicircle that the two actors, certain choristers, and Scott played throughout the production.

Act One

Victim Impact Statement

ONE and TWO enter from downstage right as SCOTT enters from downstage left. They regard each other across the bare stage, a silent moment of shared acknowledgement.

ONE and TWO turn and set their gaze on us. SCOTT watches them both as TWO speaks.

TWO: I was told I wasn't allowed to address him directly.

I had to write it down. I couldn't refer to it as something that he had done. I had to talk about it just as an event and I really struggled with that. And not being able to talk with him directly.

Pause.

All of it had to be approved, sent in to Victim Services to be approved, and the judge looks at it before the sentencing and . . . I felt like I couldn't go off of that but the night before court I just remember staring at it and thinking . . . this feels wrong, like I want to be able to . . .

ONE: And so I wrote a paragraph in addition to what I'd already submitted. And I was really kind of worried. I wasn't sure whether I was allowed to do this and whether the judge was going to stop me because it wasn't part of the official statement.

TWO: And so I got up the next morning and I remember feeling really nauseous. Mom made me something to eat. And then we all went to the courthouse in Pictou, like a ten-minute drive.

The CHILDREN'S CHOIR enters and takes their place through the following.

There was a lot of press there. My aunt was there, who I hadn't seen in a while, and it drew in a bunch of people that wanted to support me, this awkward thing. Some of his family were there. His grandmother. I'm assuming his sister was there. I've blanked that out.

The CHILD enters and pauses in front of SCOTT, attempting to make eye contact with him. SCOTT avoids his gaze.

The CHILD goes and joins the CHOIR.

And I remember wheeling into the courtroom, it being really quiet.

SCOTT wheels up to where the CHOIR is.

I remember wheeling in, and the carpet is like greyish brown. And really ugly. And I had to wheel up to the front and there was a ramp up to the mic.

Shane was sitting in the . . .

ONE: Over to my right, I guess, from where I was at the stand.

TWO: And I remember staring at the victim impact statement, the sheet of paper.

It was yellow.

And . . .

I was really scared, this completely . . . open, vulnerable moment.

And . . . I started reading.

> *ONE plays the intro to "Fljótavík" and then after a moment SCOTT begins conducting, cueing the CHOIR to sing.*
>
> *Eventually . . .*

I talked about the attack and how it caused isolation, social stigma, being separated from my friends due to my new disability. My social circle being affected by that. My family life being affected by that.

I remember talking about the piano in particular. And that was I think the most emotional part of all of it, talking about how he had taken away a lot of music for me.

I don't know if I looked up at all. I just read what was on the page.

And then at the end I decided to go off of what I'd submitted. And I read what I'd written in my journal the night before.

He was sitting there. And I looked at him.

And I started to say: "Shane, nothing can justify what you've done to me . . . "

And I remember the judge kind of inhaling, kind of like he was surprised that I was reading something other than what was on the page, and I just wanted to get the main message across, before he stopped me, so I just went right to it and I said: "Nothing can justify what you've done . . . but I forgive you."

The CHOIR *finishes.*

Something in his eyes.

Humanity.

Remorse?

Like my words hurt him. Like what I said made it harder for him to . . . to process it all. Like, if I just screamed at him it would have been easier.

And then I went back. And sat with my family.

The defence lawyer got up and, kind of, doing what they do, kinda pleading to the judge about a reduced sentence because of Shane being high and drunk. His past, all these things, and then—

He got up.

And kind of faced me.

And he said, "I'm sorry I put you in that wheelchair."

And then he said, "I don't know why I did it."

Silence.

The judge made reference to other cases to support his decision for ten years in prison. I don't remember how the crowd in the room responded to that.

But when I forgave him, I remember, on his side of the room, there was a, like an . . . emotional inhalation. A gasp.

SCOTT: No, not a gasp.

TWO turns to face SCOTT.

It wasn't a gasp.

TWO: No, not a gasp.
It wasn't a gasp.
Gasp is too strong a word.

But it was like . . . it was felt.
It was felt in the room.

Verbatim

Two CHORISTERs move to the pianos and sit down.

ONE: I was approached by this theatre director from St. John's. Jill. She suggested the idea of making a play about my story.

The CHORISTERs begin playing the intro to "Með Blóðnasir."

TWO: I had actually been conceptualizing a play myself, about the journey of the spirit through trauma and the path towards resilience and hope. In my play there was going to be a dancer, a child.

SCOTT cues the CHOIR to begin singing.

ONE: Jill said she thought it would be really powerful to have a play that had the music of a children's choir as its backdrop, and because I've worked with a lot with children's choirs in the past that I could conduct. She eventually pitched Robert as co-creator, and we ended up meeting for the first time a few months later.

TWO: I wasn't feeling too hot that day and I didn't want to go out and so I asked him to pick me up a carton of milk. He also brought coffee and croissants—and cookies. And Danishes.

ONE: I said that if we were to do this, I really needed a constant supply of baked goods, oh and to be a co-writer. And he immediately suggested verbatim theatre. Which meant the words, all the words, would be coming from me, directly through conversations. It felt right, the words coming from me. And having agency, like, in that sense.

Over the next couple of years, we ended up meeting every four-to-six months, audio-recording and transcribing our conversations. We'd read the transcripts, come back, and we'd work on it together. I'd change my mind about how to say something, or if I wanted to say it at all.

TWO: I was shocked at how many times I said the word "like." Like, a lot.

SCOTT cues the CHOIR to stop singing.

ONE: Robert said there were hundreds of pages of transcripts of our meetings. Many, many hours of recording. And even though it's condensed from that, it still feels pure. Subjective. And also truthful.

I knew these words had to be said. I wanted—needed them to be expressed. But I didn't feel like I could do it. I sensed I'd feel more comfortable having actors speak my words than doing it myself.

When people see this, I . . .

I know it's going to be maybe a shock to them. I think a lot of my friends think of me as a vulnerable person, but this . . . it's the most vulnerable I've ever been. Because there's so many things in this that I've never . . . I've never expressed to anyone.

The two CHORISTERs at the pianos return to the CHOIR.

I'm Trying to Tell You Something

TWO: Back when I was in grade nine, I looked up some porn—

SCOTT interrupts TWO, then cues the CHORISTERs to plug their ears and sing an excerpt from "Inní mér syngur vitleysingur."

Back when I was in grade nine, I looked up some porn on my mom's computer at work.

ONE: She taught at a community college, like, nursing.

TWO: And I was in her office and she left me alone and I watched a few videos.

ONE: I wasn't . . . you know. I was just watching it—

TWO: And I remember I would go to—

ONE: I didn't even know what porn was.

TWO: I was searching because a bunch of people were talking about it in my class, and I looked it up, and I was just like—

ONE: What the hell?

TWO: I was fascinated, like—

ONE: What . . . is . . . this?

TWO: All the while looking over my shoulder.
And later that week, we're driving home from school, Mom and my sisters, Sherise and Gabrielle, in the car. And my mom said—

ONE: "Scott, I found some gay porn on my work computer, and I'm just wondering if you want to tell me anything?"

TWO: And I was just—

ONE: "Mom, I didn't look up the porn!"

TWO: And it just like . . . escalated, and I was all—

ONE: "I didn't look up the gay porn, okay!"

TWO: And Sherise chimes in—

ONE: "He didn't look up the gay porn, Mom, just leave him alone!"

TWO: And that was that.
And so my mom, being the person that she is, said—

ONE: "Okay.
I believe you.
If you didn't look it up, then that must mean that a student broke into my office."

SCOTT cues the CHOIR to stop singing.

TWO: And so my mom . . . had security come in . . . to investigate the crime scene.

Pause.

ONE: It's so weird how you can live double lives. Like, being in the closet and feeling like publicly you're not gay, but then flip to page sixty-six.

TWO: And you are.

ONE: And then you close your Sears catalogue.

TWO: And you go to bed.

ONE: And you fall asleep thinking about your friend Laura and how wonderful it would be if you were able to fall in love with her and get married.

TWO: I think around age eleven or twelve.

ONE: Like thirteen or fourteen.

TWO: I knew for sure.

ONE: But then there was denial. Depression.

TWO: Like the end of grade eleven, my sister was going off to university—

ONE: And Sherise and I were so close. She didn't know and—

TWO: And I remember really wanting to tell her before she left and playing this game like—

ONE: "Sherise, I'm trying to tell you something, but I can't tell you what."

TWO: And it would be—

ONE: "Just tell me, that you know, because I'm telepathically telling you something."

Pause.

And around the end of grade twelve, I remember—

TWO: I went to the city. I travelled from New Glasgow to Halifax. To meet this guy.

ONE: I told my mom that I was meeting a friend from youth choir.

TWO: And then when I went to university, I started telling people.

ONE: I finally told Sherise by email in the fall, and she came up to visit me. And then—

TWO: I think I told Cara, my older sister, oldest sister, in the winter of that year, and—

ONE: I told my mom over the phone. I just—
Yeah, you know, that was a mistake, telling her over the phone. I have a lot of shame about that . . .

TWO: But I feel like any way a person decides to come out is the right way. They found their way, and that's what happened, and so I'm trying to practise self-love and be like, okay. And I do remember prefacing it by saying—

ONE: "I'm going to drop a bomb."

TWO: Those were my words. And it was just . . . I was crying. Mom was asking me things like, "How long have you known?"

ONE: She was being, like, really hard to read.

Beat.

And after all that, only then did she say—

TWO: "Oh.
So . . . it *was* you with the porn."

I Want to Do This

ONE plays the intro to "Viðrar vel til loftárása" on the piano.

TWO: I saw my friend playing and was like, "I want to do that." That was grade eight.

The CHILD from the CHOIR moves forward and stands next to the piano, watching ONE play through the following.

I had an obsession with cleaning other people's houses when I was younger—don't ask. And I would clean my friend's, or my neighbour's house, and in exchange she would give me pickled carrots. I would clean the whole downstairs of her house and that's what she would give me. I can't remember why I fell for that. Anyway, I stumbled upon her CD of Horowitz playing the "Moonlight Sonata," and everyone knows the first movement, but I had never heard the amazing third movement, like, incredible. And she had a big speaker system, sound system, in her house, and I think I was ten or eleven and I put it on, blasted it, and I was just so . . . mesmerized. I relistened to that movement over and over again. I didn't clean the house that day.

TWO begins playing the accompaniment as ONE speaks.

ONE: My first time performing in public was with my sister. I was in grade three, she was in grade four, and we were singing "Tell My Ma." My mom was obsessed with the Rankin Family, and she would play the CD non-stop, and she taught us that song to sing in the folk song festival. Sherise was a nervous wreck. And then we got down and she burst into tears. But we did place third, I'll have you know. It didn't really matter, they gave out awards up to fourth place. I mean who does that?

And then when we moved to Nova Scotia, my mom encouraged us to sing in choir.

ONE plays the accompaniment again and SCOTT cues the CHOIR to begin singing.

TWO gets up from the piano as a CHORISTER moves down to the piano.

TWO: She didn't force us. She would never do that. But she really kind of encouraged us.

My dad. He's a drummer. And maybe because we'd moved away from BC, and him, maybe that's why she . . .

I think she just wanted to keep music in our lives.

Summer of Scott

The CHORISTER *at the piano plays "Inní mér syngur vitleysingur" (attacca); the other* CHORISTERs *sing and sway with the music.*

TWO *starts to dance on the spot, using only his hands and arms. His movements, at first small and reserved, grow and grow until he is positively exuberant and unrestrained. He travels the stage, dancing through the following.*

ONE: Okay, Montreal, 2009, that was, like, the Summer of Scott. I met Emilio, my ex from Argentina. I was living in Montreal, after living in Winnipeg. Winnipeg! And I moved to Montreal for four months. Under the pretense of researching my master's thesis at McGill.

It's like, no, honey. No!

No, you're just going to live in Montreal and party with your friends. And we lived in this cheap-ass apartment—

TWO: That was beeeeauuutiful!

ONE: In Charlevoix. It was unreal, like four hundred bucks a month. And we would go out on the weekend and find a bar. Along Henry Street? And my friend had good DJ suggestions, and so she would come and we would be like—

TWO *encounters the* CHILD *in the* CHOIR, *and they dance together for a moment.*

TWO: Dancing!

ONE: No particular story here, I just remember—

TWO: Dancing like crazy!

ONE: And the night that I met Emilio was at this bar and it was one of those . . . They have these parties where it was like gay-oriented, but it wasn't in the Village, so it was kind of like taking the gay out of the Village, and it was the most incredible fucking night!

Because I remember just not caring about what I looked like. And of course, that's when you meet someone.

TWO moves towards ONE.

And he comes over, all rehearsed like—

TWO: "Tu es très beau."

ONE: Like over and over and over again because he speaks Spanish.

"What?"

TWO: "Tu es très beau."

ONE: And I was like, "What!?" And he was like—

TWO: "What the fuck, I rehearsed this all night."

ONE: And then he's like—

TWO: "You're really beautiful."

Beat.

ONE: "Thank you."

And then I tried to speak Spanish to him. But it was, like, representative of, I guess me letting go, of some of that armour and—

TWO: And dancing!
Daaaancing!
Wooo! Summer of Scott!

ONE: Summer! Of! Scott!

ONE and TWO spin into each other, dancing wildly, ecstatic and frenzied, the fun of youth. They run across the stage and leap past one another, their energies colliding, simmering and sensual, a moment of unabashed queer joy.

SCOTT eventually cuts off the CHOIR as ONE and TWO slow to a sway-waltz, out of breath. The CHORISTERs go still, all their eyes on ONE and TWO.

A soft, beautiful moment of this. Peace. Naïveté.

They continue to sway-dance through the following, TWO facing us, his head on ONE's shoulder.

She Allowed Me to Be

TWO: One of my first memories is dancing with my mom to Paul Simon. And the memory I have is just, like, this green dress. And seeing her feet move. I think I was three.
"Diamonds on the Soles of Her Feet."

ONE: Shoes.

TWO: Yeah, I was really young.
We were in this low-income housing, in a really rough part of Nanaimo. And I just remember, Mom would have these . . .
Mom was going through a really hard divorce.

And having four kids to take care of by herself. And . . . just taking time to dance with us?

And that is such a teaching—teachable moment for me. About the importance of taking time and . . .

And she was . . . allowing me to be. You know?
Allowing me to be me.

ONE and TWO finish dancing and, without looking at each other, slowly step away.

She wrote me a letter.

SCOTT gives ONE a folded letter.

A deep breath. ONE opens the letter and reads. SCOTT watches.

ONE: "Dear Scott.

I remember when I was young, the synonym for happy was gay. I remember my mother referring to happy moments in our home by saying: 'We will remember this as a time of gaiety.' When I was young, I knew no other meaning of the word gay.
When I think of asking you when you were in grade ten—

Asking you if you were gay. I'm sorry that you were not comfortable telling me of your struggle.

I regret that you must have gone through many years alone, and I cannot help thinking that you did not feel safe within your family to disclose your orientation. I expect that our move to Nova Scotia did not help to facilitate your openness. While on the West Coast you were in your element and then dropped into a trip across Canada. I don't know how you did it, really. I often thought the piano was your escape and also your curtain. Such emphasis was placed on athletics in your school for boys. Yet you managed every day. You managed to avoid fights and altercations, managed to get along well with teachers, to do well in so many areas, and even excelled in many. Do you even realize how resilient you are? How many times you could have become a victim or lost your sense of self or become angry, acting out as a teenager.

Beat.

When your sister Cara was born and I held her for the first time, I said to your dad: "Wow, so this is how much my mother loves me." Until that very moment I had no comprehension that mother and child love was not mutual. Not even close. So, there is no limit or boundary on the love I feel for you and your sisters. No. I'd never experienced this limitless love for any others in my life, even though I've been in love a few times over the years. So I tell you this so that you know, I carry you in my heart and soul forever. For you are a part of my very existence on Earth and in the next life as well.

Love always, Mom."

ONE folds up the letter and hands it back to SCOTT.

We Both Had Just Moved Back

TWO: If you grow up in a small town in Canada and you're gay, the goal is to move away. To the city, right? To get to a place that's safe.

ONE: I had a one-year contract

TWO: teaching ESL in Seoul. And I was moving there thinking:

ONE: Oh my god, nine million people, like,

TWO: there's gotta be . . .

ONE: But, I was working in a—

TWO: A super homophobic environment.

ONE: There's an area in Seoul for gay bars called

TWO: Homo Hill.

ONE: It's right next to where the sex workers are, tucked away up on this—

TWO: Hidden.

ONE: And the school where I was,

TWO: there was another teacher,

ONE: and he'd worked there for seven years.

TWO: And nobody knew he was gay.

ONE: 'Cause he'd be fired.

TWO: It's still seen as an illness.

ONE: And gay men working with children—

TWO: Is like—

Pause.

ONE: And so I was just like—

TWO: I cracked.

ONE: There was this final moment where I was like—

TWO: This fucking closet!

ONE: And I moved back from Seoul, kind of making peace with it and being all: okay, I actually think I could live here, in Nova Scotia, and actually do some advocacy work and go into the high schools and talk about being gay. And I really tried to move to Halifax initially when I first got home, 'cause I love Halifax.

TWO: Well . . .

ONE: Well. I loved Halifax.

TWO: As an able-bodied gay man.

Beat.

ONE: But nothing was coming up

TWO: in terms of job opportunities.

ONE: And jobs just kept falling into my lap in New Glasgow.

TWO: I had three jobs,

ONE: one as an organist, one as like a private music teacher,

TWO: and one as a server at a café . . . So it was just like,

ONE: yeah, I made peace with that and then started a choir.

TWO: Actually, the night before the attack was our first rehearsal

ONE: and we had forty people really interested in being in this choir and it was a safe place. It wasn't directly linked to social change at that point, other than like, we don't judge people, everyone is free to be themselves here.

TWO: There was a wheelchair user there that night actually, and—

ONE: And it's shameful, but I remember thinking—

TWO: I remember thinking: "How are we going to make this work for him?"

Beat.

ONE: And I remember that sparked a conversation with my friend about paralysis, and I remember saying—

TWO and SCOTT turn to look at one another.

SCOTT nods his head, as if giving TWO permission to proceed.

TWO: I would not want to live if I became paralyzed.

Pause.

I said that. That very week.

Silence.

ONE: Shane.

He . . . so okay, he was in foster care or the system. I think the system, went into juvie or something, in Ontario, and lived there, and then had just moved back that summer and I'd just moved back from Korea, because I quit and I moved home around the same time that he did and then I . . .

TWO: Encountered him.
In the bar that night.

ONE plays "Fjögar píano," a small moment of music that drifts into silence.

Nobody Told Me

TWO: We were celebrating my friend, Andy, his art gallery opening. I was really on the fence whether we were going out or not. Like, I just remember feeling pretty tired, because I went out the night before. But in the end, we decided to go. And—

Oh.
I just got this weird memory. Of what I was wearing. I was wearing this, like, plaid, button-up shirt, and then on top of it, this light blue wool cardigan.

Which I never saw again.
For obvious reasons.

Beat.

We went to the art gallery, and it was like, a bunch of friends. And afterwards we decided to go to the Acro Lounge. And we got there, and we ordered beer, and we were dancing. And crappy radio songs and shitty disco lights, and upstairs there's a bunch of pool tables and the bathrooms. And my friend Amy went upstairs to the washroom and I kind of followed her. I think I wanted to talk to her about something, and I got to the top of the stairs, and I shouted her name really flamboyantly.

And that's just the way my twenty-seven-year-old self . . .
I just remember being . . . a lot more gay. Which is strange to say. Maybe society beats the gay out of you over time. Anyway, at the time I was like, "Ammmmy!" Just as I was meeting eyes with this guy.

I remember him with a small group of people, standing by the pool table. And I remember it was like everything happened at once: I shouted Amy's name, then I was also . . .

I was sort of checking this guy out.

And that's not really something I tell people. I think I hesitated to tell people, and felt weird about it, especially considering what he did to me. But it was just a moment like . . .

"There's a guy."
"Is he cute?"

And I remember him looking, meeting eyes with mine, and it was just . . .
I recognize that look.
I don't want to be up here.
I don't feel safe.

And so I turned around, and I went downstairs.

Pause.

Probably like forty-five minutes later, and Andy and I, we were walking down the street. We have a very chummy relationship. He's straight, but we kind of had that type of friendship, so I had my arm around his shoulder because I was helping him walk, because he was pretty drunk. And we were walking, and we just heard this shouting. And Shane and his friend . . .

And honestly, when he came up to me, he was so . . . bizarre. Like scary, but I wasn't scared. He walked with such a strut that he was doing this weird—it was a mix between basketball, like dribbling a ball, and . . . dancing.

I was just like: Okay.

And then he came up behind me and he tried to cut my throat.

Pause.

I think I went into shock. Because I don't remember when he did this. But I do remember that he said something in my ear.

And then I fell to the ground. I remember that moment, falling to the ground and sobering up and being like: Okay. And not being able to move my legs, and looking over and seeing Andy realizing I'm on the ground, and Shane's friend saying, "It's cool, man, it's cool," and Shane is gone.

And then one of those shots in a film when you just see . . . you're looking up, and people's heads come over you, looking down. And one girl is like, "Oh my god." And it's a very weird thing because people are drunk, Andy is drunk, this girl is really drunk, and they are kind of just . . . observing.

And then the police come. And the ambulance comes. And the whole time I just want my legs to be straight, because of the way I've fallen, I've fallen with my legs under my hip, and I'm trying and can't . . . and I'm telling myself: Oh, the wind has been knocked out of you.

The ambulance ride is just a rush of lights. Lots of orange lights. And I'm really trying to breathe through it. And I'm feeling my grandmother's presence, which is so bizarre. Feeling like she's close to me.

At the hospital, everyone is trying to call my mom. Constantly calling her and she just won't wake up. And they finally get a hold of her, but she's thirty minutes away from New Glasgow, so she . . .
Her foot is heavy on the pedal.

At the ER there's a bunch of doctors and nurses. They have to take photographs for evidence, pictures of my back. And that's when . . . I feel something running down my back, and the police officer who's behind me, she faints.

And I'm like . . . police don't normally faint, do they?

Is that blood?

Have I been stabbed?

Beat.

Because I didn't know up until that point.

No one really told me.

ONE begins to play the intro to "Dauðalogn." A CHORISTER moves to the piano, eventually replacing ONE.

SCOTT cues the CHOIR to start singing.

ONE and TWO stand in stillness and watch him conduct.

After a while:

What's So Gay?

TWO: What's so gay about being in a choir?

ONE: Singing. Using your voice.

TWO: Right.
But being in a rock band is not gay.

ONE: Singing with other boys is not the issue. It's being in a choir.

TWO: Right.

ONE and TWO watch SCOTT again as he conducts the CHOIR.

Eventually:

But why though?

ONE: Well . . . it's not as aggressive as a rock band. It's more . . .
It's about . . .

TWO: Beauty.

Beat.

ONE: Yes.

TWO: And singing high for a boy is gay.

ONE: And even in a choir, you know, it's like more gay to be . . .

Beat.

TWO: And men don't dance.

ONE: God no.

TWO: That's like an expression of your inner feminine side, to dance, right?

ONE: Part of it. And I feel that's like—

TWO: It's like the gayest thing.

ONE: Yes, and that's why men don't dance.

TWO: And you have to keep your elbows below your shoulders.

SCOTT's conducting gestures slowly rise throughout the rest of the scene.

ONE: Right?

TWO: As soon as you do this *(puts hands above head)* you're—

ONE: Gay.

TWO: Right.

Beat.

Right.

But now . . .
That's like—

ONE: That's mostly what I do.

SCOTT cuts off the CHOIR. His arms remain suspended in air, above his shoulders.

The Key

TWO: The second or third night in the hospital, I got a Facebook message from this person I didn't know, admitting who had done it.

ONE: I didn't know her. She just looked me up on Facebook. Because I was in the media.

TWO: And it was a weird intro, where she described herself.

ONE: That she's a single mom, that she went to such and such school, and that she was a server at this bar, and—

TWO: "I'm the twin sister of the man who attacked you."

Beat.

Weird lead in.

ONE: And I didn't know where it was going. But then I was
like, Woah.
She went on to talk about him. His upbringing, his history.

TWO: She said she wasn't justifying what he did, but—

ONE: "Just so you know, he's struggled. He's been in and out of the system, the supports just haven't been there."

TWO: Just so you know.

ONE: "I love him. But I hate what he's done to you."

Pause.

I took screenshots, sent them to the police. And then I wrote back and said—
"Thank you for reaching out."

Silence.

TWO: My mom.

ONE: She's just a very forgiving person. Empathetic.
Nurturing.
She taught us some really important lessons.

TWO: Through being a single mom. Husband struggling with alcoholism.

ONE: Protecting her children. It was a really close-knit family and we learned so many important things through that process.

TWO: She put us first.
She was like, no, my children are more important than this.

ONE: Dad's a beautiful man. My mom taught us that too, you know. She didn't pass on anger towards my father.

Pause.

People come up to me and are like—

TWO: "How many years did he get? How long is that asshole in prison?"

ONE: After getting that message from Shane's sister, and also having the mother that I have . . .
Like, hearing that piece of the story was the key for me to shift my focus and be, well, why did this happen?

Why did he slip through the cracks? Why was he neglected? Yeah, it's his mom and his dad, but how did they get like that? And what are the conduits, the channels that we create in society, through shit like toxic masculinity, misogyny, white privilege, and homophobia, that put him on this track?

Beat.

TWO: "How long is that asshole in prison?"

ONE: That attitude is exactly why that asshole exists, you know?

SCOTT motions for the CHOIR to move downstage and sit on the floor.

The CHILD curls into a ball on the floor behind SCOTT's wheelchair.

Five Months

ONE and TWO sit on a piano bench. ONE plays the intro to "Straumnes."

SCOTT cues the CHOIR to start humming the music.

TWO: I was in the ICU, I don't know, for like—

ONE: I'd say a week.

TWO: And then I was put in the step-down unit, the intermediate, you know what it's called—

ONE: The IMCU.

TWO: Intermediate Care Unit. And then—

ONE: A week and a half or so on the main floor of the hospital.

TWO: And then transferred to rehab, where I was for three and a half months. Which could have been longer, a lot of people stay for six months or more. But the whole hospital stay was five months.

Pause.

And there's like so many moments. I remember—I remember that the shock was just . . . constantly there. And they were trying to figure out my medication. At one point my legs started to spasm. Because I have an incomplete spinal cord injury, which means there's still nerves attached and—neurogenic bladder. And the pain started to set in so they were trying to manage the pain. And trying to eat lunch. And my

family would come visit me. And I couldn't be around them. Because I could feel their pain. And it made me feel my pain even more.
And just crying.

SCOTT indicates a brief pause in the music.

ONE: Lots of crying.

ONE plays "Fljótavík" on the piano. SCOTT cues the CHOIR to begin gently singing.

TWO: Headphones.
Listening to a lot of music. Sigur Rós.
Ugly sobs, doing my best to be silent.
Four people in the unit. Separated by a thin cloth.
And they had to put a central line into me. Because of the amount of blood that was lost.
In case they had to do a transfusion, and I had such a panic attack about that, like— This is what they do for chemo and leukemia patients, and they had to give me Ativan for it because I was so terrified. And after everything I had been through, that was the thing that . . .

Pause.

And in the ICU, I was in there for a while. Because the spinal cord had been severed, some of the spinal fluid started to leak out of the spinal column. And it kind of created a little bubble, and they knew that because— Because every time they tried to elevate the bed, I'd start projectile vomiting, and I couldn't stop. So they had to do a spinal tap, put a catheter into my spine, which sounds terrifying but—

ONE: It's extremely terrifying.

TWO: Even the slightest amount of infection that gets in there can go to your brain and cause brain damage, and so I was petrified. And I had this young Newfoundland doctor, this resident doctor, who was, like—

ONE: So fucking hot.

TWO: My whole family was so enamoured with him. I just remember he was—

ONE: He wasn't cocky.

The CHOIR finishes singing and they watch ONE and TWO for the remainder of the scene.

TWO: But he said this in a way that was so self-assured, and reassuring, he said—

ONE puts his arm around TWO's shoulder and imitates the doctor. TWO quietly plays the piano as he listens to ONE.

ONE: "We need to do this.
We can either do it tonight while I'm here.
Or it can be with someone not as good tomorrow.
When I'm on vacation."

Beat.

TWO: And I was like— *(enamoured)* Oh. My. God.
And he's all like—

ONE: "It's up to you."

TWO: And I just remember being like, "All right.
I'll let you do this.
Because you are cute."

Beat.

TWO finishes playing.

He was a really, really good doctor, you guys.
Such a good bedside manner.

Don't Be Afraid

ONE moves next to SCOTT as TWO plays the intro to "Ára bátur." SCOTT cues the CHOIR to start singing.

Eventually:

ONE: People in New Glasgow organized a benefit. For my recovery.
And my friend had six different designs, rainbow designs, for a button.
And she was like, "What is the message you want to be on this button?
What do you want people to go away with from this event?"

And I just remember thinking about . . . fear.
And thinking about how many decisions in my life I've made out of fear.
And how afraid my community was at that moment. And my family.
And how afraid I was, about my life. With a disability. And being gay.
And I was just like, "No Fear!"

But then we realized that was like a skateboarding clothing line in the '90s. And so we said, "Don't Be Afraid."

> *The* CHOIR *begins to gently weave around the stage, in single file, as they sing. Some of the* CHORISTERS *touch* SCOTT*'s shoulder as they pass by him.*

And then another friend started a photo campaign. She painted the button design on canvas and went around the city asking people to pose with the sign and she uploaded those photos to Facebook and it really took off.

And I remember being in the hospital bed and seeing all these photos from around the world coming in. Every continent in the world.

And media, CBC, Global. The first interview I did was in rehab with the CBC, it was two months after I was attacked. I think it was Anna Maria Tremonti. And it was on *The National*, my story was on *The National*, and then I think George Stroumboulopoulos posted about it and Dan Savage spoke about it at one point and it was in, like, definitely in American news and international news. And people would reach out, a lot of people from the States. Some people over in Europe. And that photo of me in Costa Rica and the hammock.

Where I'm in a grey-white tie-dyed shirt with a beer in my hand lying in the hammock? That did the rounds to the point that like I—
I ended up dating a guy from Texas.

> *The* CHORISTERS *form a protective circle around* SCOTT. *They quietly sit on the floor before joining hands with one another.*

And it was, it was exciting, you know? I think it surprised me. Part of me was like, oh my god, people care. And they're engaging with the campaign. And being energized by the energy that people were giving me.

And the hospital staff, I'm sure, hated me at the end of it because there were too many people in the room and people in the waiting room.

The CHOIR slowly rises and moves into formation in front of SCOTT. The music swells, building to the end of the scene.

I remember the power of it, and it was just a wave of love. You know, after this horrible moment, the worst moment of my life, it was just a wave of love passing through those hospital doors, and carrying me on and out. I just felt like I was riding this wave of love.

Beat.

And so we formed a proper not-for-profit. And then Vox, our choir. Vox started having events on social justice issues, not just queer issues.
Rape culture, misogyny.
Sex positivity.
Mental health.
Racism.

Beat.

When I was deeply in the closet in high school, and like—
Clinically depressed.
The piano was what I turned to.
Choir was always this safe haven.

This place that could help me process who I was.
And express who I was.
Where I could be my most authentic self.

The CHOIR finishes singing.

ONE looks at SCOTT.

The power of choir.

SCOTT: Yeah.

ONE: Don't Be Afraid.

Dear Scott

SCOTT hands ONE a folded piece of paper.

ONE: This is a letter that I wrote myself in 2014, a year after the attack.

Dear Scott.

In October of 2013, you will be out, celebrating.

A young man will whisper something in your ear. He will try to slit your throat. He will stab you in the back.

You will try really, really hard to move your legs.

You will tell yourself: I need to breathe because if I don't I will disappear into my fear.

You'll think: I can't live like this.

Pause.

Here is my message to you, Scott: Don't be afraid.

You were so afraid growing up. You were afraid of yourself. Your stomach hurt, your heart pounded.

But soon you will start to see life from both sides—before and after. You and him.

He is also afraid. He has lived in fear and insecurity. He has been failed—by the people in his life, by his community, the system. And the result will be an act of destruction he can never take back, two lives that will never be the same.

Beat.

You'll ask: Can I do this? Will I be able to do this?

Everything in you will want to say no. But you will try, you will risk. And you will leave it all on the dance floor.

You will come to understand the difference between hope and shallow optimism.

Beat.

And you will choose love over fear.

ONE folds up the letter and gives it back to SCOTT.

This Story

TWO: I have a weird relationship with this story. The story of that night, the attack. The aftermath.

Sometimes it's fine. Telling it. Even cathartic.
Other times, it really affects me.
Like, not in the moment, it'll hit me like a day or two later.

I don't know. It's interesting to revisit it, so many things that you forget about until you're retelling.

Like the sweater. They just cut it right off of me when the paramedics came.

Beat.

I ask: Why did all of this happen?

ONE: A lot of people think that I shouldn't be exploring that question.

TWO: People say, "Maybe it was just completely random."

ONE: That I should just accept that it was random, but New Glasgow is one of the poorest towns in Canada. It's rated number one worst town to live in, three years in a row, by this magazine, like—
Three years in a row. It's a steel town. And the steel factory shut down and caused a lot of damage to the economy.

I rarely saw any diversity in New Glasgow. Isn't that messed up? There's a very segregated Black community up near Brown Street, just, like, contained. By the way, Forbes Street, where I was attacked, was right next to the Cabaret, the same building where years ago Viola Desmond was fined and removed from the theatre because she was Black. The class difference in New Glasgow is very stark. It's just one or the other, you know?

And there's a middle class, but there's a lot of rich people and then there's this really poor population. Smaller towns around New Glasgow: Stellarton, Thorburn, really poor. Trenton.
There are a lot of shootings in Trenton.

There is a lot of class difference and a lack of diversity in Trenton, too.
He's from Trenton.

Beat.

TWO: People say, "Maybe it was just completely random."

ONE: But if we're talking about the years that led up to this, this is not random. And if we just dismiss it as "random" then we're missing the root causes: social injustice, poverty, hopelessness, toxic masculinity, white privilege, and hate and anger and homophobia.

And if we dismiss the root causes, then we are not going to learn anything. And it—
It can't be in vain.

The CHORISTERS hum a B-flat 4 drone (a cappella), seamlessly entering one by one. The drone/cluster pattern oscillates throughout the scene, creating a haunting, unbroken thread of sound that underscores the words of ONE and TWO.

Beat.

TWO: I feel like I'm tethered to that sometimes. The decision that day. To forgive him.

A story being public. Once that gets sent out to the media, and how you forgave your attacker, that's all they know. Its uncomplicated, they just see the one narrative. The one narrative because it's easy to understand.

ONE: It's a good narrative.

TWO: Yeah. That hopeful narrative about forgiveness.

Beat.

ONE: There were days when in the media I was so empowered by the love that was encircling me. And it was so liberating.

TWO: But there were also days when—

Pause.

—someone messaged me on one of the dating apps.

The CHOIR hums a two-note cluster.

The message popped up out of the blue, and I didn't recognize him. I didn't know who this man was, and yet he obviously knew me, my story, from the news and media coverage, I guess, because he said: "I bet all the attention has gone to your head."

The CHOIR hums a three-note cluster that intensifies over the following:

It was the only message from him that I saw in the chat box, but he implied that he had been messaging me for weeks.
"I'm doing you a favour, hitting on you, ya know. The least you could do is respond.
Crippled asshole, I'm glad he attacked you."

The CHOIR *returns to the unison drone, gradually opening to an "oo" vowel.*

Beat.

And I was doing dips at the gym. And I usually kind of throw myself backwards into my seat, when I'm finished doing the dips, and I just missed the edge of the seat and fell a stupid distance, like two feet. And my tailbone, it just cracked.

The CHOIR *sings the two-note cluser ("oo").*

People with spinal cord injuries tend to have osteoporosis below the level of injury and—
And I just flipped from feeling really healthy and active to being not healthy and mentally very unstable and I was smoking all the time and . . . and I was just so angry at . . .

The CHOIR *sings the three-note cluster ("oo") that opens to an "ah" vowel, full volume.*

Like a surge of anger, like I hadn't felt before, welled up towards him. You know?
Like, oh right, RIGHT! Osteoporosis, of course, you think, okay, I could stop there, but it's like, no I also have osteoporosis from the waist down now because of what you did to me.

The CHOIR *sings the unison drone ("oo"), closing to a faint hum.*

Long pause.

ONE: From the moment they told me I'm not going to walk again.
From that moment to—
The moment. In the courthouse. The victim impact statement and the . . .

The CHOIR *hums the two-note cluster.*

TWO: Eight months.
It was just eight months

SCOTT *cues a brief three-note cluster, hummed.*

Pause.

I do feel like I'm tethered to it sometimes. That decision.

The CHOIR *gently hums the unison drone, with a slight crescendo towards the final line.*

Beat.

ONE: I am tethered to it.

TWO: But I know . . .
I do also know that—
I can cut that cord.
Whenever I want to.

Beat.

I do have that ability.
To just say to him: No, not anymore.
I'm sorry.

Pause.

I'm sorry, Shane.
I don't forgive you.

The CHOIR *stops singing, inhaling on the cut-off; a quiet yet intense release.*

SCOTT *looks at* TWO *as they fade into darkness.*

Act Two

Before and After

Lights up.

SCOTT alone on stage in front of a piano. He looks at it silently for a moment, and then he begins to play the opening aria of the Goldberg Variations, BWV 988.

He plays alone for a while and then TWO enters, watches him, and then eventually:

TWO: It's hard to describe the importance of the pedal for piano.

The one you use most is the sustain, and it just opens up the sound. It prolongs the . . . when you depress it, it just creates a richness, a warmth.

I miss that warmth. I miss the music that requires that pedal, I miss it with a searing passion. Beethoven, and Brahms, and Debussy—all the music that came after this . . .

Beat.

This is the aria from the *Goldberg Variations*. Bach. It was composed for the harpsichord, an instrument that had no pedal.

But on the piano, resonance can be achieved by holding chords, and then anything you play above or below will sing more . . . will spin. You don't need the pedal.

It's a very old style of dance in which the middle beat is emphasized. A transitional beat that you lean into that takes you somewhere unknown.

It's just, like, such a simple little piece but in it I hear all of my life, ya know? . . . the pain and beauty, the unexpected, the hard transitions—and joy—that I've come to know . . . the grace and wisdom those transitions reveal.

Beat.

Before I was attacked, I dug into this piece and practised it for hours on the piano, without the pedal . . . and without truly understanding the meaning it would hold.

Now these waves at the end, rolling onward towards the final dissonance, it's inevitable resolution. A resonance that doesn't need my foot against the pedal to be sustained.

It is the piece I can still go to, that I love the most, and that remains the same now as it did then. A link between the before and the after.

Forgiveness

ONE: I want to meet him.

Beat.

I want to meet him.
And—

After I was attacked, I just had this urge to get a sense for who he was, and part of me, I think from the beginning, I was like: I want to know him. I really feel like that is a more beneficial thing, restorative justice, for his processing of this, for his learning from this, if he sees the effects of what he did sitting right in front of him.

Beat.

I sensed that he was just a . . . scared little boy. In the sentencing, seeing his face, I did feel like there was this . . . I don't know.

Beat.

I googled the word forgiveness. And . . . I stumbled upon this woman. This woman who wrote about her father being murdered.
Her father moved down south somewhere, and his gardener, I think, murdered him, and stole from him. And he went to jail for life. And at a certain point, when she was much older, I think she was maybe seventeen at the time, and when she was in her thirties, she was contacted by this man's lawyer, and it was really bold. He said, "This could really help with his healing, and this could help with him getting out of jail. Would you be interested in restorative justice?"

And she thought about it, and she said yes, and flew down there with her family. And went through this process.

TWO: And I was like . . . fuck.

ONE: And she's in BC. And I wrote to her. I wrote to her and told her that I was really moved and that I'm in a similar situation.

And when I went to BC we went for coffee, and it was the . . .

Beat.

I was expecting it to go so much differently than it did. I thought she was going to be really pro-restorative justice. But she was like:

TWO: "You need to know . . .

You need to know that this can't be done to accomplish anything.

It's not something that you can have any expectations for.

It's messy. It's painful.

It is something that is really hard, and complicated, and—"

Beat.

ONE: My psychologist said:

TWO: "You should wait to meet with him until you just can't wait any longer. And you just know, for certain."

ONE: And then I'm like, okay—

TWO: Do you really want to meet him? Because I think deep down inside I'm afraid of meeting him but—

ONE: But he gets out in, like, a year and a half. It was a ten-year sentence, and—

TWO: And I would be really nervous of meeting him if it was in prison. But if it wasn't in that context. If it was just us outside of prison and I randomly encountered him on the street.

ONE: Then I think that would be . . .

SCOTT cues the CHOIR to sing "Debata mandire" (a cappella).

He's way younger.

TWO: He was nineteen and I was twenty-seven.

ONE: And he was big then. But now . . . I see pictures of him. And . . . He's been working out.

TWO: He's like, massive.

The CHOIR finishes singing.

Hi Shane

TWO plays the intro to "Varúð" (attacca).

SCOTT cues the CHOIR to sing.

ONE: "Hi Shane,

I'm not even sure if you check this account. I've been wanting to reach out to you for a while. I think about that night all the time, maybe you do too. Tonight's a pretty painful one, thinking about how my life has changed since. I've been thinking meeting with you might help me work through the pain. I'm not sure if this would be something you're open to, but I wanted to try. Let me know what you think."

SCOTT cues the CHOIR to stop singing. ONE begins to play the piano, a brooding, bass ostinato that grows heavy.

TWO moves around the stage; he paces, back and forth, consumed in deep thought as ONE plays thick, oppressive chords on the piano.

SCOTT cues the CHOIR to sing throughout the following:

TWO: "Hi, Scott. This is Shane's friend. I'm sorry to hear you're having a hard time. He told me he's not sure if he's legally allowed to have contact with you. But he would be willing to grant your request if there was a way to go about it. Perhaps through his parole officer at Dorchester. Kind regards."

Pause.

ONE: Dorchester. In New Brunswick. One of the oldest penitentiaries in the country.
Attempted murder.
I've driven by it. And known people who worked there and it's just like . . .

TWO: Grim.

Beat.

The CHOIR, one by one, begins to rhythmically pound their fists against their palms, then stomp their feet against the floor.

ONE: Yeah. Grim.

The music grows in intensity and darkness. The CHOIR suddenly charges downstage towards SCOTT and stops right in front of him.

SCOTT cuts off the CHOIR and keeps his hands suspended, covering his head as if shielding himself.

Flamboyant

ONE: I bite my hangnails.
Like, you can tell how stressed I am according to how bad my fingers are.

TWO: Obviously.

ONE: And there are times when I just, you know, peck away at them, peck away at them—
Nothing big.

TWO: And then other times when I'm like full-on cannibal.

ONE: So I can trace that all back to grade four. In Nanaimo.

TWO: This bully of a teacher.

ONE: And it was just horrible, like, he would consistently give grief to all of the boys who would do poorly in math and he would favour the girls.

TWO: In a gross kind of way.

ONE: And then when it would be gym time— Because he taught gym as well. It would be all the boys that would shine.

TWO: And I was not one of the boys that would shine in either.

ONE: And I just remember that experience, and . . .

TWO: Gym class was always a scary time for me.

ONE: Grade eight. And having to go down in the locker room with all these, you know—

TWO: Horny, creepy, pubescent...

ONE: ... boys. I was in the corner, like, oh my god, I don't want to be seen.
And that's what the bullying was always about, you know, it's always about me being effeminate or ... you know?

Beat.

Like, faggot.

TWO: Obviously.

ONE: Got called that a lot. Baseball, gym class, and that teacher, he would say things like:

TWO: "You run like you're a girl."

ONE: I just remember that starting to stick. At about grade four.

TWO: You run like a girl.

ONE: And so that's when I started biting my hangnails.
And I haven't stopped since.

Pause.

TWO: After I came out, I used to like the fact that I had straight male friends.

ONE: Like, it used to really make me feel—

TWO: It would separate me from—

ONE: Because at that time, gay culture was still really—

ONE: I mean, there was no *RuPaul's Drag Race*,

ONE: which is just—

ONE and TWO pop their tongues, paying homage to the show.

TWO: I would love the fact that I had straight male friends, and—

ONE: And every time I talked about being gay it would be as a joke.

Beat.

To make people laugh.

Pause.

I'm still trying to get rid of that.

TWO: There's always that internal dialogue, toxic masculinity, and just telling myself, "Okay, don't be really gay."
Like when I talk about that night, describing how when I got to the top of the stairs and yelled my friend Amy's name out, every time I describe it, I was "flamboyant."
Why is that labelled as flamboyant, why is that—?

Pause.

Before we started creating this show I had that idea of doing a play myself. I had a few specific ideas about it but the clearest notion I had was of a dancer. I miss dancing like I used to. It's a very basic human and primal need to move however the fuck you want.

And so, the image I had in my head, of the dancer for my play, was this kid.

TWO turns to face SCOTT.

That little gay kid inside me, the one the world made so afraid to just move. To dance. He's right there, smiling at me. Unknowing of what is yet to come in his life. The happiest little boy you could ever meet. He is about ten years old. Nature lover, soul singer. But this little kid, he is also a dancer. Of the purest form.

ONE plays an excerpt from "Ára bátur" (B section).

TWO begins to slowly sway then turns round in a circle with his arms stretched up to the sky. He is overcome with joy.

Spinning, twirling, the sheer and utter joy for life. When I see a child dancing like that, it's like I am breathing air for the first time, the freedom and immensity of the spirit inside. The spirit within, finding its way out. At long last.

The music plays out as TWO finishes his dance.

He's Up For It

TWO: He can do it.

ONE: He can do it, and he's up for meeting with me because—

TWO: He said because he feels he "owes it to me."

SCOTT conducts the CHOIR as they sing "Varðeldur" (a cappella).

Beat.

Yeah. Not necessarily because he wants to, but . . .

ONE: It's like—

TWO: He's moved on from this.

But he feels like he owes it to me.

ONE: He said he would meet with me and, I think it was in relation to meeting with me that he apparently also made a point of saying—

TWO: He said that he didn't do what he did because of homophobia.

Pause.

ONE: Obviously he has the right to—

TWO: But I'm processing the anger, like, you don't get the right to say . . . to do this to me and then say I'm lying, you know?

Beat.

ONE: Part of me is angered by that, but I know that that anger is . . . I don't know, not irrational.

TWO: It's totally rational.

ONE: But it's—I'm just like—

TWO: Why? WHY?
He gets all the power in that sense, and it's frustrating.

Pause.

I don't want to do it. I don't want to meet him, if we're going to get in there and he's going to start going into— If it's going to be an argument, you know? If he's just going to blame the alcohol, or—

ONE: Because in my head, I'm like—

TWO: Who would admit to that, right? A hate crime. And see, that is really scary and frustrating because—

ONE: I was hoping this meeting would bring about something more than an argument and this—

TWO: This is really testing my forgiveness.

Pause.

I go to his Facebook page every now and then. It's chilling. There are a lot of people just like, "Can't wait till you get out."

ONE: That day, when I forgave him, you know . . . his relief—

TWO: He said something to me. I don't know what he said and—

ONE: And when he apologized.

TWO: I don't know what he said and I didn't want to say it was "go to hell, fag," or whatever because . . . I don't remember.

ONE: When he apologized there was just this sadness. This humanity, and—

TWO: As he was cutting my throat. Stabbing me in the back. I don't know what he said to me.

ONE: I just really feel there was this kid, this little boy, that had been neglected.

TWO: Part of me wants to ask him. But meeting him in real life, nothing can prepare me for what would happen in that room.

ONE: There were two little boys on opposite ends of the knife that night. And those two boys, they could be anybody.

TWO: It could be really retraumatizing. Once I meet with him, I can't undo it.

ONE: And when you have two kids like that, you know, which one is it going to be?

TWO: I can't undo that.

ONE: Which little kid is going to be on which side of the knife in fifteen years?

SCOTT cues the CHOIR to stop singing. The CHORISTERS walk to the lip of the stage, forming a line that faces us.

TWO plays the intro to "Untitled #1—Vaka." The CHOIR begins to sing, unconducted.

One by one, at staggered intervals, the CHORISTERS slowly step backwards, leaving the line.

The line gradually disappears, until there are only two boys isolated in light near the lip of the stage: the CHILD and another boy. The piano accompaniment ends and they sing together for a moment (a cappella). When they finish singing, they turn to face each other and stare in silence.

Eventually, the CHILD takes a step back and leaves the other boy. The boy turns out to face the audience, looks at us, utterly alone.

The CHILD turns back to the CHOIR and is beckoned by a CHORISTER whose arm is outstretched towards him. He slowly walks back to the group and into the arms of the CHORISTER who beckoned him. The CHORISTER embraces the boy and cradles him while humming the final line of "Untitled #1—Vaka" like a lullaby. Some of the CHORISTERS nearby place their hand on the boy, a moment of profound connection.

Through the Knife

ONE: So when the judge sentenced him to ten years we kinda all sat with that. And I remember leaving the courthouse and being surrounded by CTV, CBC, Global just asking about it and I was so relieved that it was over and that he apologized and that I'd forgiven him and that really unlocked a lot in me and I wasn't aware of it at the time. But I just remember my demeanour was different than when I entered the courtroom. I left being able to breathe a bit more.

And then we went outside of the courtroom. Spoke with my aunts and my mom. Someone from his family. And later seeing it on the news that his grandmother said . . . basically admitted to his homophobia. And then we went home and . . .

It was a sunny day. It was beautiful. I think it was June 8, 2014, and my friends had come up, a few of them, and Sherise, my mom, Gabrielle, and Cara.

And we were all just sitting around in the driveway. With like a glass of wine. Just kind of unwinding and . . .

Beat.

Everyone else was kind of getting things packed up and Mom and I were out on the deck. Mom was on the deck. And I went out . . . she started to cry. And one of the things she kept repeating was that she . . . she was just trying to live her truth as a mother. And she was so hurt and like . . . I've never heard that information from my mother. She kept grabbing her chest saying I'm just trying to live my truth and I want to help you.

I want to help you.

And I just was so angry and everything unravelled and all of my pain was being thrown at her and . . . and I just snapped and—

TWO: *(furiously)* I need to be able to take care of myself! I am not a child and that is what I feel like. I feel like I'm a child again! Twenty-seven years of becoming independent and it's like I'm a baby again. At twenty-seven! Learning how to . . . navigate the world, learning how to piss and shit and . . . have relationships. At the hospital, they knew when I had a bowel movement before I did sometimes. How embarrassing is that? They would have to . . . I'd have to rely on the nurses to catheterize. And it just feels so . . . gross for me to rely on you, Mom! And for you to know so much about my . . . personal details, because you're a nurse, and Cara's a nurse, and you know what's affiliated with . . . these personal things, like you know way more than I want you to know, and you are . . . !

Silence.

ONE: I don't know how that conversation ended.

But it was like a huge contrast to that day, just . . . what I had left the courtroom feeling.

Beat.

I mean obviously it wasn't going to fix everything, forgiving him.
And . . . and it clearly didn't.
And it shifted things and I knew that I needed space from Mom but I didn't know how to tell her that without punching through the wall.

Which . . . is exactly what I did.

Pause.

That trauma that he went through. It passed through the knife. And it affected my relationship with everyone in my family.

Mersey River

ONE begins to play the intro of "Andvari" on guitar, soft and beautiful. TWO listens for a moment, then speaks.

TWO: Mersey River is such a special place for me. In Nova Scotia, in Kejimkujik National Park. I've always been there during pivotal moments, it seems. And I was home, there with Mom during the pandemic lockdown. And I was like, this is where I'm meant to be. And being there and using that time to connect with my mother. And talking about things, laughing with her, and just healing in that way had been really amazing.

And it was June, it was just after my birthday . . . And Mom and I went to Keji and she was at the beach and I wanted to go for a hike. And I received this call when I was catheterizing in her car. Because there were no accessible bathrooms available. So I was in the car catheterizing and saw this phone call and voice message and I knew this is . . . Mom is usually the one who has no caller ID, but she had left her phone in the car so this is not Mom.
And I just felt weird about it.

Pause.

And then I went hiking and I decided mid-trail that I was going to listen to the call.
So I stopped to look at the view, and decided to listen to the message.
And it was from Correctional Services.

And what a fucking name, by the way. Correctional Services. We're correcting people. Great.

ONE cues the CHOIR to start singing.

Beat.

Anyway, it's this woman, and she's relaying this information. And at one point she . . . I don't know, had this brain fog or whatever, and messes up and says something, I forget what it was, but then she started laughing in the middle of this very serious message about him being released on Wednesday.

ONE cues the CHOIR to stop singing.

Pause.

And I heard it.
And then I hung up.
And I just sat there and I was like . . .

Pause.

I knew he was getting released. But I don't think I ever really fixed the dates in my mind. Like June 10.
So when I finally got the date, it was just two days away from when I got that voicemail. And . . .

I wanted to meet him, you know, to help me work through what I have to work through.
But then he was released, and the likelihood of that happening was suddenly very low.

Beat.

It was just a wave of uncontrollable emotion.
Another layer of grief.
And just . . . sobbing profusely on this trail.
Looking out at this just . . . beautiful . . . place.

Do You Forgive Him?

A CHORISTER *plays the intro to "Straumnes II."*

TWO: I'm finding it's harder to forgive people who you know.

ONE: A friend that you're really close with and you fall out of friendship with them because they've done something that really hurt you and you haven't been able to express that. And you also can't let it go or forgive them.

But then I can forgive him.

And I'm like: Why?

SCOTT *cues the* CHOIR *to start singing gently through the following.*

Pause.

TWO: I didn't know him.

ONE: Yes. Like, with people that you have a history with. There's so much . . . .

TWO: It's like in Buddhism they talk about—

ONE: There's a Buddhist monk, Thích Nhất Hạnh, who talks about the knot. The knot that you have, and the longer the history, the bigger the resentment, the bigger the knot is.
And the more entangled it is.
And the harder to . . .

Pause.

TWO: Sometimes . . . I feel that knot. With him.

ONE: And I don't know him.

TWO: But in a way I do. Because it's been almost nine years, and he's still a part of my life every day because of what he's done.

ONE: And there are days that I still forgive him.

TWO: But there are days that I don't.

TWO makes a decision.

ONE and TWO turn and look at SCOTT.

ONE: Scott?

SCOTT stops the CHOIR and turns to look at them.

TWO: Do you forgive him today?

At this moment in the show, SCOTT would take the time to answer, expressing his truth for that given day. For the purposes of this publication, we have included a version of his answer as delivered on March 10, 2023, during the run at the National Arts Centre.

Today's a really, uh . . . emotional day and maybe this is just the way it feels after ruminating on this question for some time, and getting up every morning thinking about it . . . It's a day when it felt harder to . . . I couldn't really seem to grasp a clear-cut answer to that, even though my response to it is so often like . . . it's quite a grey answer most of the time and I never really settle on a yes or no, because it's such an *impossible* question . . . but, today I'm overcome with emotion just being able to bring this play to life with this incredible group of people, and being able to perform it for this incredible town, that's really held this story and this um . . . the message, which is really important . . .

It's really interesting to think about that question, you know, and the various ways that that question is asked . . . How forgiveness is asked of you, or of someone else . . . I don't think I've ever had anyone ask me, "Can you forgive me?" "Will you forgive me?" And that, like . . . it's . . . it's almost a little bit ludicrous. And whenever I've heard that phrasing before, it's felt so, like . . . inappropriate . . . putting someone on the spot in that way . . . but it's a different thing, though, for you to ask, "Do you forgive him?" . . . because both of you represent the parts of me that are grappling with that question . . . and this is something I ask myself every day now. . .

It struck me today that, you know . . . that I'm not sure if he ever wanted or asked or wondered if I would forgive him . . . I think he was in a place of, like, just . . . *such* hopelessness. And I don't know him, so this is me speculating . . . But anyone that does something of this magnitude . . . I believe that it's just a really loud cry for help. And one, you know that . . . A behaviour like that, you know, isn't . . . I don't think that's genetic. No, I don't believe that . . . I think that's a behaviour we foster by ignoring it, or over-punishing it, or encouraging it through larger issues like toxic masculinity, homophobia, or misogyny . . .

I think that's something we can all agree we've been sucked into at some point or another, and that forces us to live a lie as gay people . . . and more generally as human beings . . . this affects all of us . . . I don't think he even went beyond "I fucked up, I've done something so terrible and I'm just a horrible person" . . . We need to show love, we need to share love, we need to, as hard as it may be, we need to express love when we *really* struggle with someone . . . And I'm saying this during a time when I'm finding it hard to show love to certain people in my life . . . I'm a total hypocrite and I'm a total Gemini . . . But this is a moment for me to just remember that and remind myself of that.

We can all do this. I really believe we can all create a world where people can make mistakes publicly, even big ones, and, like, not feel so ashamed and punished to the point of isolation or self-hatred, to the point of harming others simply because of who they are. Let's hug them harder, we can love each other harder before we let it get that far. . . I'm just thinking of that little kid in all of us; in me, in you, and in him. And how we all deserve to be loved harder and hugged closer by one another . . .

A CHORISTER vamps the opening bass line of "Untitled #3—Samskeyti" on the piano throughout the following scene.

The Same Person

ONE: I've been thinking about it when people ask: Do you feel like you're the same person?

TWO: And I'm like, I don't know.
I don't remember who I was before all of this.
But now. To a lot of people. Now I'm often defined by my forgiveness.

ONE: But forgiveness is such a personal thing.
But I don't believe in generalizing forgiveness. Making it into this thing, like in Christianity, where "we must forgive."

TWO: When you feel like you are drowning in an ocean, all this pain and trauma, that's weighing you down, and pulling you down . . .
Because you're like, I need to let this go, because I'm getting pulled to the bottom.
But there's also vulnerability associated with knowing yourself to say "I can't forgive." I don't think there's anything wrong with that.

Beat.

ONE: I think when you can forgive . . .

TWO: And when you can't . . . you're doing it to survive.

ONE replaces the CHORISTER at the piano and plays the full intro to "Untitled #3—Samskeyti."

The CHILD moves to TWO and stands on his feet and they start to dance, sway. SCOTT watches them dance for a moment, then moves to the lip of the stage.

TWO leaves the dance, sits at the piano, and plays the accompaniment with ONE for "Untitled #3—Samskeyti." SCOTT cues the CHOIR to begin singing.

The CHILD continues the dance, picking up momentum as the music grows in intensity. The CHILD breaks into a dance, something unleashed, joyous, and completely untethered. When the CHILD finishes, he walks down to SCOTT as they both turn to face us. The CHILD sits on the floor next to SCOTT's wheelchair. They look at each other, and then out at us.

The end.

Alternate Response for Scott

TWO: Do you forgive him today?

At this moment in the show, SCOTT *would take the time to answer, expressing his truth for that given day. For the purposes of this publication we have included a version of his answer as delivered on August 27, 2022, during the run at the Arts and Culture Centre.*

I never seem to have a revelatory answer to this question. I seem to always be in the middle . . . But today I woke up, and, well . . . there's this scene in the play that, every time we get to it, it really gets to me . . . after they, um, sing in that line, and they . . . they walk back one by one and . . . until there's one boy left and he walks back and someone holds him . . . someone rocks him and sings him a lullaby . . .

Each time it . . . it makes me think of this notion of resilience. And how we always think it's a . . . like, an individual thing and if you can overcome your struggles you're "resilient." And it's on *you*, and *you did that* . . . But if we could just think of resilience as a communal effort like what we witness in that scene. People loving people even when they've done something horrible . . . Not trying to correct them, not trying to fix them . . . but trying to understand why and trying to love them anyway . . . I wish we could embrace that version of resilience and understand people from that perspective and I think that had we done that with . . .

There's this saying that we all know: It takes a village to raise a child. But it also takes a village to neglect one, to ignore one deliberately, in such a negative way . . . Why, so early on, did we give up on him . . . why was he forgotten so much, to the point that he attacked somebody? Seeing that scene over and over again and the way it continues to affect me deeply, it's like, "Why?" What he did . . . it was him trying . . . that was him getting to the point where he had to hurt someone so horrifically just so that he could be seen, so that he could get help . . . and he didn't get help, he went to prison. And we all know that doesn't help anyone. We all know how that goes . . .

That's kind of been on my mind recently. I'm still really angry at him for what he did to me . . . And I'm also really angry at all of us for giving up on this child, this beautiful kid, who deserved a village of people looking out for him. He didn't enter this world with hatred for others, so what happened? And what does this act of violence *truly* mean?

Acknowledgements

Admiralty House Museum, Zoe Allen, Sarah Antle, Jennifer Arkin, Sue From Baked, Caitlin Bowers, Carolyn Boyes, Marion Brown, Andie Bulman, Hannah Cameron, Erin Casey, Finley Cavanagh, Brandon Cave, Jessica Chapman, Sarah Churchill-Goodman, Annette Clarke, Mary Fay Coady, Sarah Conn, Ann Connolly, Kaia Cormier, Jean Paul Courtier, Andrew Crawford, Andy Cunningham, Stef Curran, Holly Daley, Diana Daly, Rachel Davis, Tanya Davis, Chris Dearlove, Lori Dolloff, Hugh Donnan, Adrien Doucet, Erin Enguehard, Alanna Fitzpatrick, Colleen Fraser, Matthew Girard, Brianna Gosse, Zack Goudie, Emilio Grosso, Maria-José Grosso, Victor Grosso, John J. Hanlon, Lesley Hartman, Christine Hennebury (AAMP), George Hodder, Nadine Hodder, David and Karen Hood, Darryl Hopkins, Andrew Iles, Blanche Isräel, Darlene Jackman, Cara Jones, Martin Jones, Ronald William Jones, Sherise Jones, Dahlia Katz, Aly Kelly, Amanda Klein, Jesse LaVercombe, Martin Ledrew, Leah Lewis, Aaron Loeppky, Dan Loeppky, Ruben Loeppky, Fiona MacAdams, Mildred MacDougall, Sammy MacDougall, Angus MacEachern, Mabel MacEachern, Yvonne Manning, Charlotte Marchesseault, Jenna Marks, Ricky Martin, Sidra Martin, Lauren Matheson, Matt Matheson, Colleen McCarthy, Janet McDonald, Sarah McDonald, Heather McKinnon, Corrie Melanson, Amanda Mews, Suzanne Mullett, Ben Murphy, Charlie Neis, Carmen Nieva, Kiersten Noel, Judi Pearl, Jamie Peddle, Katharine Petkovski, Cynthia Peyson-Wahl, Elizabeth Philpott, Flora Planchat (Canary Cycles), Edna Pletchetero, Jessica Power,

Amy Punke, Annelie Reimer, Katie Roux, Graham Scott, Claire Simmons, Elsa Simms, Justin Simms, Ralph Singh (Universal Music), Darren Smith, Robert Smith, Terra Spencer, Peter Standbridge, Mary-Helen Stevenson, Elizabeth Sweeney, Steve Topping, Bill Voisey, Aaron Wagner, Gabrielle Waugh, Lloyd Waugh, Lois Waugh, Laura Marie Wayne, Shannon Webb-Campbell, Phil Winters, George Woodhouse, Kevin Woolridge.

Scott Jones (he/him) is a musician, filmmaker, writer, and activist who is passionate about using creative expression as a way to build bridges with people and communities. After surviving a homophobic attack in 2013, Scott was compelled to use music and artistic expression as a vehicle for positive change. With the help of his loved ones, Scott founded the Don't BE Afraid campaign and facilitated VOX: A Choir for Social Change, advocating for the rights of queer people and raising awareness about the very real and dangerous repercussions of queerphobia. For four years after the attack, Scott worked with the NFB and filmmaker Laura Marie Wayne to create the award-winning documentary *Love, Scott* (HotDocs, 2018) about his experiences with small-town homophobia and violence. Since that time, Scott has written and directed live action, music, and animated short films that centre queer and disabled perspectives, including *Coin Slot* (Best Atlantic Short Film, AIFF, 2022), *Freedom*, and *Good Samaritan*. Scott has also trained and worked extensively as a music facilitator and choir director, having conducted the Nova Scotia Youth Choir (resident conductor), the Pictou District Honour Choir, and Vox Populi. He has guest conducted the Amadeus Choir, Shallaway Youth Choir, Lady Cove Women's Choir, Mount Allison Choral Society, and Singing Out LGBTQ Choir. For his artistic and advocacy work and for his community engagement, Scott received a YMCA Peace Medal, a Nova Scotia Human Rights Award, and a Mount Allison Alumni Award (Contemporary Achievement). Scott has a Masters of Arts from the University of Toronto and a Bachelor of Music (Piano Performance and Choral Conducting) from Mount Allison University.

Robert Chafe is a writer, educator, actor, and arts administrator based in St. John's, Ktaqmkuk (Newfoundland). He has worked in theatre, dance, opera, radio, fiction, and film. His stage plays have been seen in Canada, the United Kingdom, Australia, and in the United States, and include *Oil and Water*, *Tempting Providence*, *Afterimage*, *Under Wraps*, *Between Breaths*, *Everybody Just C@lm the F#ck Down*, and *The Colony of Unrequited Dreams* (adapted from the novel by Wayne Johnston). He has been shortlisted three times for the Governor General's Literary Award for Drama and he won the award for *Afterimage* in 2010. He has been a guest instructor at Memorial University, Sir Wilfred Grenfell College, and the National Theatre School of Canada. In 2018 he was awarded an honorary doctorate from Memorial University. He is the playwright and artistic director of Artistic Fraud.